LET'S FLY TO TRAZODONE: Poetry By Miriam Stanley

- A Single Volume.
- 120 pages.
- Trade Paperback.
- American contemporary poetry collection by a single author.

Contact Information / Order Online:

http://www.roguescholars.com

Design and Layout by C. D. Johnson

Front Cover and Frontispiece: New York City graffiti by artist unknown

ISBN: 0-9840982-6-7
ISBN13: 978-0-9840982-6-2

Published by Rogue Scholars Press
New York, NY - USA

HiSS

24 HO
ELECTRO
PROTECT
ECUR
URITY SYST

718-726-

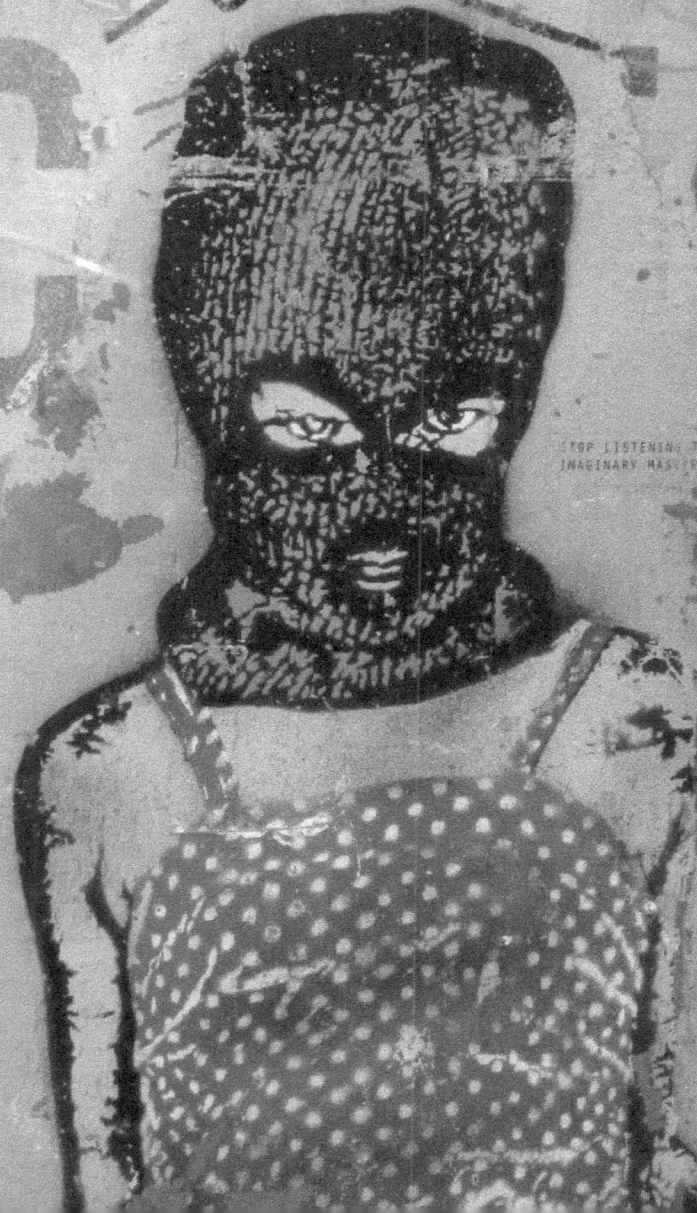

STOP LISTENING TO
IMAGINARY MASTERS.

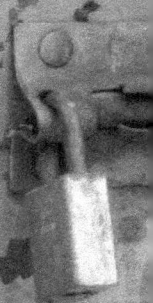

Let's Fly To Trazodone

Miriam Stanley

Published by Rogue Scholars Press
www.roguescholars.com

Dedicated

to

NV, XS, Rema, Ethel, and Connor

–

Special thanks to

Iris N. Schwartz

Editor

LET'S FLY TO TRAZODONE - Table Of Contents

Table Of Contents Continued...

APPENDIX

Publisher's Page

Rogue Schoolars Press Books In Print

FOREWORD

My friend Miriam Stanley messaged me a request: she wanted me to write a foreword for her new poetry collection, "Let's Fly to Trazadone," and include information about how, when and where we met. This is a difficult task, because I feel like we have known one another forever. She could be the first cousin who got into trouble with me at my grandmother's Brownsville home when I mixed up the meat and dairy knives, or the second cousin once removed who practiced dance steps with me on the porch.

Maybe I met Miriam at the Yippie Museum Café or the Shout-Out at Otto's Shrunken Head. Both of those venues, and many more, are gone now, but we are still at it. There is a realism and narrative that we share in our work, artistically and professionally. We both believe that art is transformative and have practiced creative therapy as a healing tool in the hospitals in which we have worked. Naturally, any services that address the soul rather than the funding are hard earned.

Miriam and I have stood together on the steps of the Municipal Building during an Occupy Wall Street permitted march and overheard a police lieutenant order his officers to clear us out. It was decision time – get busted or raise bail. I can't be arrested again – been there, done that, too many times – so I watched from the perimeter, writing the number of the Lawyer's Guild on my lower arm, as an officer named Cohen arrested Miriam. You could clearly hear her screaming "Shondah" at him as he led her into the waiting paddy wagon. I felt like a wimp and a bad friend – if she was going, I should have been going, too. We laughed about it when she was released several hours later.

Miriam and I have read one another's work, featured in the same venues, and traded books, as we wrote them. We have commiserated about the future of poetry as well as the present, while working on the annual Alternative New Year's Day event or trying individually to delve deeper into the writing, make the unspeakable loud and clear. We have read poems in Zuccotti Park and the Bowery Poetry Club and ABC No Rio. We have grown.

Miriam has always had a certain dry humor in her poetry, as well as an historical sense. In reading the new work, the personal experience has become one with the vision. She is writing as it is, as it was, and as it will be, against a backdrop of Jewish culture mixed with clubs and clinics and cats. And, of course, the city in which we live. It is a New York City poem, "Becoming a Native New Yorker," that brought me a line I wish were mine, both literally and in spirit.

When strangers ask where I live, I say "in celebration."
Don't worry, Miriam. I will credit you when I steal it.

- Puma Perl

AARP CARD

Get the early bird special!
Plane tickets!
Broadway shows!
Get discounts on bicoastal chains of Denny's!
This is the special pass to marked-down life!
It lets you know that although you're losing vision and
hearing, and you resemble a vampire without your partial,
you are now FLUSH WITH CASH: EVERY DAY IS BLACK FRIDAY!!!!
Get consoled by cut-rate facials!
Visit a New Jersey spa named Whispering Beach!
Eat a plate of Caption Ed's!
Take a trip to the sauna!
Get lavender hand cream, 20% off, at KMART!

In these last, tired years of stints and bone density trials,
be the first person seated on the plane!
Demographic royalty!
The woman who books cruises to Cancun and
Bermuda, then tastes everything at the salad bar low in
sodium!
You don't have to stay home and lose your mind.
Lose your mind in sunny Florida!
In a Spanish-tiled rental.
Or in a plush movie theater that shows matinees.
Live to the max!

AGING CLUB KID

When teenagers laughed,
I stopped dancing.
Exiled Doc Martins to Goodwill.
Hid my Lycra in a drawer.
Aged from nymph to matron.
Wore wool, and terrycloth slippers.

When I recall
the Limelight, Nell's, the Palladium,
the labyrinth of stairs, and streams of techno,
the crowds frenetic on the floor;
women dancing in cages from the ceiling,
palaces of desire and want,
my insides twitch like kittens caught in
a bag of nylon mesh;
children locked in a dark room.

ALL THAT AND A BAG OF CHIPS

Sixty and divorced,
wearier than a donkey,
the work week fleeing behind,
a pack of cigarettes stuffed in the shirt.
You're heading out to get laid;
maybe, eat some dinner.
It is Friday: FRIDAY NIGHT(!)
A sabbatical in your arms beautiful as a woman.
The city is twenty miles ahead and you have to get parking...
Night closes in;
it is six o'clock in January,
getting fun takes so much trouble.
The snow melts against old tires,
fantasies flare up,
the libido cracks its whip;
you explore the Jersey Turnpike: a modern Ulysses
passing every Exxon.
A widow waits in a hot room, drinks cappuccino.
She is your target.

BACK ON THE MEDS

I am like the man who won't count his sons,
I hide hope from the devil.
I can speak of the bad years:
The run of insomnia.
Lost promotions.
Being a reckless pain-in-the-ass.
The divorces before
I rescued myself.
That day, I stopped skirting the emergency room,
finally entered an office.
A therapist came out;
I got the doctor's scrip.
Joined a community you might not know.
A fellowship without steps or rooms.
Where names are well hidden.

Now, I take my dose.
Go to work.
Build a rep
as a stand-up colleague.
And like the prodigal son earning a second chance,
boredom is a relief: perfect as clean underwear, a book with all its
pages.
I run steady as an airport.
Survive crisis by knifing through the waves.
I kiss each breakfast in daily reunion.
And keep cautious when things are good.

BALLAD OF THE ANOREXIC

My hipbones are wings, the belly a bowl,
I float above mediocrity,
honed to the sharpest point;
it took eighteen months of sit-ups,
a thousand hours of running.
I am Ayn Rand, a Nietzsche acolyte,
an "Ubermensch,"
I won't buy a TV;
won't EVER relax.
My weight flickers hottest blue.
Four inches of space are between my thighs.
My mother ate lamb chops, gnawed their bones,
slammed the dishes;
in the bedroom I counted my ribs,
each one: a rung leading out of the house.
Menstruation once bloomed like cancer, like a stroke.

BARE

You see my linoleum peeling like sunburn.
The Venetian blinds missing slats.
You buy Kerman rugs
and etchings.
But I am the one who owns a state-of-the-art divorce.
I am a book of rules.
I own a timer and a bell.

Paradise is a big-ticket item.
I love you with every part of myself,
but you can lose it all.

I slough off men and property like a busy womb,
a murderous loner,
a ship with ballast;
you might be a
detail in a busy year.

BARLEY HARVEST (Song of Ruth)

I

She is uprooted,
scattered;
possessions blown away,
the son, father
peeled off.
She drifts with dust in the roads off Moab.
The mother-in-law sleeps in front.
A cart with linen is all they have.
April roams with dogs.
Her life is winnowed.
Soon she will glean what others reject.

II

In the valley east of Beth Lechem, workmen wave their sickles.
Then tie sheaves out of the heart of loose stalks.
The poor walk behind,
glean the remnants in promising patches.
It is a parade of the desperate, a passage to hope;
G-d walks behind them, doesn't sing.

Soon the sheaves are gathered into wagons rolling into the barn.
The straw burden is brought to the threshing floor.
Beth Lechem aches in sleep.
The hills of Judah are lush and breathing.

III

Daughter-in-law,
loyalty,
love.
The labels sewn like saddles to asses.
She travels on them, eats dried dates, she is
in the wheel from old to new.
Chemosh is a god she throws behind.
Kir-haresh is a forgotten city.
She is no longer the pagan from an enemy land;
she is the immigrant in love with modesty.

Only a man can complete her.
And even then, he must provide her with child.

IV

Does she think about tile,
the finery, the silver she once had?
Does she think about Orpah, her best friend back home?
Does she remember the soft feet of royalty?
Now she's on the threshing floor, talking to a local man,
taking the final step in the harvest of her life.
He says, "Maybe,"
he "...has to think about it."
She curls up in the stone of waiting;
she is barely ripe.

BECOMING A NATIVE NEW YORKER

I found a city job in Flatbush.
Snuck a cat past my landlord.
Learned to say "fuck you" in Spanish.
Got chased by dogs in Far Rockaway.
Turned grey, got divorced.
Lost a co-op.
I learned that
shop stewards are avenging angels with cell phones.
And the head of DC-37 is a schmuck.

I sold my chametz* to a Buddhist nun.
I read novels at the Barnes and Noble
of Union Square without paying.

I have erased eighteen years of Jersey.
Kids getting stoned behind the 7-11.
Endless miles to find a library.
Browning lawns with rusty lawn chairs.
I now call bridge-and-tunnel an "acute disease"
and upstate: a place to die.

When tourists finally returned after 9-ll,
I yelled, "Thank you!" while chasing the bus.
When strangers ask where I live,
I say, "In celebration."

———————

* Chametz is leavened bread, which is sold or given away by Jews
before Passover.

Miriam Stanley

BODY

I flung you into fistfights.
Betrayed you to young men.
Threw you, almost, into the street.

Perennial victim: diets starved your jaw of bone,
pruned the teeth of calcium,
I polluted the blood like a public garage.
Made muscles jump like monkeys.
Throughout college, I fainted at subways.
Helped up by clerks in newsstands,
offered sips of orange juice.

I've spent hours of panic waiting at the 9th Avenue Clinic.
Once got tested in Harlem,
compared earrings with a kind, transgender phlebotomist.
How you withstood coffee binges,
weeks of popcorn,
handfuls of Tylenol.
How your wreckage became an archive of words:
poems called "Dentures" and "Ringworm."
Your destruction more treasured than a room of gold fillings.
Now, I get to sleep at dusk.
Huddle in fresh sheets.
Wiggle toes in pockets of warmth.
I'm more organized than a casino,
safer than lip balm.

My abused possession:

I brought you back
from the front,
Brought you back from danger and dirt.
Finally.

BRADLEY BEACH

With Barney sneakers, they stomped ants to bits.
Chased seagulls with fries;
scared a sick pigeon whose skull was cracked.
Your ex walks behind, slathering lotion from a bag.
Talking to her boyfriend.
She asked the kids if they would like Yoo-Hoos.
Her thick legs, plodding on the Jersey shore.
They said yes, after pointing to some strangers
they called "retards,"
then jumped into her SUV.
Eight bags of Cheetos later, the brood – your kids – shouting
over video games, twitching their thumbs on pixel
Kalashnikovs, vigilant as tweakers searching for meth, call you up.
Their greetings bulleted with demands.
"No," they answer, "we didn't visit the museum.
We can see a dinosaur on a smart phone."

Miriam Stanley

THE BRONX IS BURNING, 1977

"Arson is a barometer of urban decay."
                - Former Deputy Fire Marshal John Barracoto

How to tell your aging mother, numbers on her arm like an old TV,
about benzene and matches lighting up basements?
about halting the school year for *niños* with books?
of burning out tenants like bleach on an ant?
of arsonists with beepers, getting your orders over the phone?

How to explain the spell of fire insurance?

She only knows Auschwitz,

not abuelas scrubbing smoke-stained dresses.
not the old men taping singed Baptism papers.
not the families doubled up in Concourse apartments.
Not the stripped copper pipes that got you even more profit.

She doesn't see Fox Street underwater,
Vyse raining down flame,
the 35,000...35,000!...alarm bells in the dark.
The Pontiacs dumped with discarded pets.

She is elsewhere. Dreaming of dead people serving her cholent.

You keep her North.
By carpeted rooms, mosaic foyers, tended shrubs. Protected
like Tiffany glass on Bronx Park East.
Yet still whimpering in terror during the Yom Kippur War.

How to tell the truth to someone who's known too much?

CASHIER

He was ordered to go downstairs.
Then enter the back office.

The gun was a surprise;
they had already got the money.

Soon, he lies there,
flaccid as a grandmother's breasts,
then solid with the hours.
Detectives find him dead,
a supplicant
far from church.
They do the chalk lines
then mutter
"G-d damn."
Later, his face is on the news;
his landlady cries while feeding her kid.

He gels into a mountain of memory:
rallies, shrines, and marches...
neighbors holding botanica candles.

Flowers dropped with apologies
at the place where he worked.
Far from Juarez,
he blooms.

CENTRAL PARK, JUNE

I saw all the young brides,
all the young grooms, too, the mothers
poured into lavender dresses.
The wind rose.
The laughter of parents
circling like sharks,
while I dunked in the
shadows beneath a bridge.
Today you are packing;
folding love
back into boxes.
Like the womb of
us, a final rewind,
while here in the park,
new couples chatter,
their hopes, like the skaters,
hover like rain on
the edge of the
bandshell.

CHALLAH

I dusted the countertop with flour.
Smacked down the dough.
The shape round and greased, walloped
the counter; the Formica shuddered,
air pockets collapsed like overused mines.

I took the glob and
tore it into six chunks.

Then, I rolled chunks into strands,
wove strands into a plait,
braised the sculpture with egg whites.
I brought the loaf
to an oven lit at 350.
The heat billowed, a chuppah*
over kitchen linoleum.

Later, I carried the yellow loaf,
like Abel and his fruits,
on the altar of a paper plate,
placed before a computer programmer;
his body first touched by me three weeks ago in
a Rococo wedding hall.
He smiles, cradles the offering like a newborn daughter.
That was on the coldest day,
of the coldest March,
in a Kollel* apartment
in Far Rockaway.

_____

* A chuppah is a Jewish wedding canopy.
* Kollel is a program wherein the husbands are subsidized to learn
Torah, instead of seeking employment, while raising a family.

CHEST HAIR

I see them in white.
Bent antennas under my lips.
I crawl on your chest, straining past sleep.
Turn to you, a turtle about to nest.
You like beneath, locked into quiet.
A futon holds you in place.
I slide across, dock my head against
the crux of your arm.
Lift my face: a membrane against the light.
I try to trust you.
Bead my tongue in the
flat border emerged from bone,
the fabric of your skin
yielding like sand,
the expanse of chest
waits like a delta underneath
my short visit.
I think of penguins.
how they incubate eggs,
passing their cargo
back and forth over the ice.
You now hold what I'm protecting,
stop the fragile from dying,
keep it in darkness
from the glare of noon.

CHICKEN

I remember, at the Wingate sidewalk,
The cat shaking like a wind-up doll,
Its fur molting on the cement,
Its meows muted, almost silent.
I stood with students on their way to high school,
Saw the kitten falling over and over,
Trying to pick herself up.
The girls said it was too late;
Rat poison got to her.
Animal Control would gas it.
And the cat,
The tiny stray,
Lay martyred,
Next to Styrofoam slathered in Popeye's
Dropped by the teens earlier in the day.
The kids walked on.

CODE PINK IN CAIRO

First, we gather in the square.
An island in the middle of traffic.
Cars zoom in dusty chaos.
The smog lifts her dress.

A travel agency.
Tea shop.
Hallal KFC.
Across the wide road.
We move to the circular platform.
The leader rises.
Blonde.
American.
Someone lifts her bag like a chalice.
Inside are maps dotted with Haifa and Tel Aviv.
Each labeled Palestine.
A crowd surges,
grabs the freebees, peels off the plastic strips, presses on
T-shirts the stickers declaring the end of a Jewish state.
A blur of announcements.

I dodge the cars, weaving through lanes, running back to the hotel.
Lock the door of the room.
Search for the ticket home.

CRIMEA, 1924

Men slip off shirts, trousers, underpants.
The women pull out hair pins.
The Red Army boys slosh through pebbles.
The Black Sea is luminous cobalt,
smeared lanolin stops the salt's burn.
The swimmers sing on the hike back home.

How easy to flourish, hidden
in the big toe of the Ukraine:

The kolkhoz* grows past its quota.
The peaches are heavy, the day is hot.
Livestock clamber in their cattle pen,
a row of lemons grows south of pogroms.
Safety is sealed, a fugitive away from pain,
the revelers scamper back to chickens, pigs, wheat.
Cows loll in fields.
Tartars ride past on wagons,
the glow splash of pink light
glides over five chickens getting their throats slashed.
- a blessing is said in Hebrew
and five women with one man pour scalding water over
the wings to ease the feathers out.

It is five full years before these Jews are sent to the gulag.
Sixteen before an ice pick splits Leo Trotsky's head.

Now the girls crack almonds, slice citrus,
the boys stir slop for the pigs,
three men trudge back from threshing grain,
the floor packs with mud,
later to be washed.
Someone mutters "shmutzig*,"
but continues to crack shells in her seat.

Fifty kilometers from Kiev,
a boat ride away from Turkey,
a packed bag and steerage away from Zion,
endless weeks away from Moscow,
a newcomer gets letters from Brooklyn.

19

She writes back. "The soviet is changing life; everything is getting
better."

At night comes the cleaning, the
sewing cloth, and women boiling eggs,
the lull of a sizzle on an iron grill,
the onions browned beige to sienna,
the kitchen fills with warm soot,
a skillet packs the bodies of five hens.
Lenin, in Moscow, is being pumped with alcohol.
His extremities oiled and smoothed,
doctors strive to pinken decomp.
Over 100,000 people paid respects.
Stalin orders Krupskaya quiet,
she yells something is terribly wrong,
that the leaders are meant to be humble.

But now it's time to wash.
One man and two women.
The pots and the dishes,
everything battered and chipped,
the dream newer than the parts,
and it is 30 forks and 30 knives,
wiped dry as sunlight.
Men go to sleep to rest till dawn,
a boy throws egg shells into the compost,
a man says Shma* in the cricket's dark.
The cows are silent mountains.

_____

* Kolkhoz is Russian for a communal farm.
* Shmutzig is Yiddish for filthy.
* Shma is the Jewish prayer said before sleeping.

THE CAT THAT JUMPED THE FENCE

Now he starts at me.
From the patio.
Back after six hours.
A bloody scar on his head.
A look that tells me he'll try it again.
All the other cats are tame.
They stroll in circles, loll in sunlight like bubbes.
But David lives by his name.
Ready to fight Philistines behind the wall.
Ready to kill all Goliaths.
His tail swollen as a penis.
He eyes the barbed wire lining the fence,
the metal that scraped his fur.
After two hours, he walks in.
Lies on the bed.
Whines for chicken.
The real king danced in the streets while his first wife sulked.
I keep my male locked in the rest of the day.
I am a tougher woman.

THE CATS GET RINGWORM

I thought the spores would wreath my head,
a crop circle on my scalp,
that aliens and birds would target me.
that toddlers would be drawn to this letter O,
that it would grow to the size of a yarmulke.
I would join Hester Prynne
and Typhoid Mary.

That a constellation of fungus
would keep me from work,
away from children, slithering plague.
I would pollute tony blocks of Fifth Avenue;
I would be scarier than bedbugs on the subway.

But no –
the fungus spread to my arm,
just the size of a quarter,
its hot-pink circumference was covered in Band-Aids.
I went to work, explained what I had,
my boss warned the spores would
float into my panties and
I would get jock itch.

My stress level reached Code Orange.
I slept locked in the kitchen,
my cats slept in the bed.
I screamed, "You're going to the ASPCA!"
They lolled on the quilt,
spreading infection like butter.
In two weeks, the circle faded to pale pink,
almost half-erased.
I drank Odwalla juice,
popped antioxidants,
detoxed from Starbucks.
I never got jock itch,
or even athlete's foot.
I washed my hands with bleach
in the sink.
Disease packed its bags,
toted off panic,

left me to sleep locked in exile
only seven more days.

My cats dipped twice in sulphur
were clean as matches,
the boiled sheets: ready for all of us.

DEATH OF MY GOLDFISH, METHUSELAH

Two days of this:
His body listing starboard.
His gills: open sores.
Food clinging to the moon of his starving back,
like confetti.

His tail splintered to hanging strings.
Without rudder, he drifts.

Fungus wraps the wrecked eyes;
he nuzzles the glass when he hits the wall;
he is the blind grasping the hard edge,
in a sea of quiet.

Bearing down on the pane of cold glass,
he stops himself from floating to his death;
fear rallies in the wake of fatigue;
nature forgot to kill him, so he waits...

Under the watchful eyes of owner and
G-d, he gasps, terrified.

DELIBERATIONS OF A BRUTALITY CASE, 1997

A smirk...
That's what I told them;
the cop had a smirk.
The jurors stared at me;
I was the second youngest of them;
a fifty-year-old looking like cousin Barry
cooed, "You must give him the benefit of a doubt."
All of us.
All eight of us brunettes.

All Latino or Jewish;
no whites on this jury;
no black folks neither;
we're chosen from a "giant" (gene) "pool."
We argue back and forth,
but no one is screaming.
We skirt the fence of decision lightly.
Finally, at five, it's, "OK, let's find the cop guilty of something...
we'll acquit him on the other offense."
And then out the door,
passing the plaintiff at her seat.
Middle-aged woman sitting down.
Wrinkled, brown fingers
holding a bible.

DINA

A baby carved out at forty.
Cancerous breasts at fifty.
Later, the solar plexus cracked like a lobster.
Surgeons sew the aorta under a rubbery grip;
masks, scarves: blue-green, aquatic linen under chilly light.
The family pacing in pairs in their imaginary ark.
Later, you return to work, bitching about parking spaces, time
wasted, the silver hair shorn for a quick morning routine.
The milk-white scan of morning report.
Your salt taste of impertinence, slipping out of meetings at wide-
angled noon.
The world under close inspection.
Ultrasound, six months, checking for fear.
You stay up at night: a pill waiting to dissolve.
All the repairs future/past - a mobile of knives.
You spoon a husband back from a long separation.
Entertain dying in his arms;
a silver lining of relapse.
His muscles lean ovals holding tight.
His eyes red sunken living rooms.
A witness of what you were.
You think of that skin flap cut from the belly, pirated onto the
chest, how everything corporal moves in time.
That of oneself and the frame of marriage.
The Buddhists say the only thing constant is change.
We just want to hold the pieces.
You kiss that man's bald head.
Fall into blindness: a doll.

THE DIRECTOR

An empty nest taunts you at home.
Now you face your wayward husband by yourself.
Employees clutch timesheets.
None will be your friend.
You tried to treat one as a daughter,
but she wrote you a memo.
Gone is the countryside of Guyana.
The church where you used to kneel.
The relatives numerous as jackfruit.
You are now the distant cornice of management.
We celebrate birthdays with you,
but eat lunch away.
Your commands and orders are protected memorials
made of stone.

THE DISLOCATION OF GRIEF

1.
Snipers plagiarize the Bible.
You grab your suitcase from under the lights.
Young girls tower,
tall as panic.
Europe is an angel or the Devil himself.
Your cities are emptied,
property grabbed,
communities roll through rain.
You're corralled to a field.
You comfort your mother.
Whole households move to a camp.
Quick: Tell me, are you Arab or Jew?

2.
Choose the right to return, the right to remain.
A future or pity.
There are riots on the streets.
Paranoia slips off her rubber coat, then there is a gun.
Armed men bang on the entrance, occupy your block;
you hoist arm onto your lap, sit by the doorway.

3.
In Tel Aviv, the mothers wear tank tops.
It is 40 miles from Gaza,
two steps from ice cream.
A soldier kisses her father and gets on a bus.
You walk to the market.
There is sun on the security guard.
You open your bag: he checks for explosives.
It is almost the Sabbath; soon the venders fold up their wares.
This is as far from bullets as you can get.

4.
War planes
missiles
checkpoints
curfews
torture
prisons.

Settlements rise on the confiscated land.
Hebron Jews break the windshields of Arab cars.
There are 500 checkpoints on the West Bank.

To subsist with death,
building tunnels and walls.
Each military post.

5.
A warren of rockets that can kill children.
Quick: Tell me again, or you Arab or Jew?

6.
It is the excitement of a birthday;
the kinder* are out in full costume.
The revelers play in the streets;
there are no Qassam rockets.
In Rafah, 10 miles away, a little girl is covered with phosphorous.
She is a well of agony with boils on her skin.
The IDF flies above like locusts.

7.
A chrysalis of Israeli soldiers;
a Hamas maze of sharpshooters.
The Mideast twitches in its sleep.

8.
You are going home.
New York is nine hours away.
You unpack your prayer book.

————

* Kinder is Yiddish for children.

DRINKING AGAIN

I.
Your arm like a fence.
Your chest, your shoulders,
the bar of a carnival ride.
I am propped up, like
Jesus before his disciples...
and mingle with guests.
You are bolstered by my social graces...
I lean on you, drowning
while I smile.

2.
Someone offers meat from the grill.
You offer coffee and look concerned.
I want you alone, without cups or saucers.
But I take it, say thank you in a gentle voice.
I drag my legs upstairs to use the bathroom...
This is the third barbecue while being drunk.
I think three's a charm and envy your wife...
the marble of the hall and kitchen.
There's another glass awaiting
my lips in the dining room.
I will forget your hands – those thumbs, fingers,
the swirling curves rubbing her neck.
Forget that lingering kiss while she lights
the birthday candles.

ELDERLY MODEL

Smooth shoulders heaving up.

Flattened breasts hanging down.

Skin tenting the fleshless bone.

Wrinkled sheets of concave stomach.

Ninety pounds...
Balding pubes...

She stares into our amazement.

Still,
So much taut,
Young skin around the collarbone.

You know the husband touches that first.

ELEGY FOR JACK WILER

Imagine a life pared down, free of mortgage and children,
duties stripped like a Shaker chair till one becomes a tourist of
other families,
watching babies and spouses displayed like small-town flags,
jotting the stories down after a neighborhood picnic.
What was it like for Jack?
Who lost his porch, the house, the crowded living room?
Missed his wife and washing the Camry;
what was it like when all those trimmings were taken away,
when what's left are worried friends,
days of vomit, visiting nurses,
and an occasional night out when T-cells bounce back?
Jack made me love backyards and bicycles,
proud wives showing off their foyers;
the cleared drainpipes and full garages,
noisy Thanksgivings and lights streaming winter through the wired
trees.
He praised what others scorned: the loud,
sticky kids and wailing infants.
He put the rest of us hipsters down a peg;
he did not mock Christmas sweaters or frosted hair,
or even the comb-overs;
he thanked G-d for each day alive.
He realized that belonging to someone is not the icing but the
actual three-tiered,
red velvet cake.
It is the tchotchke* dusted with the love of a good parent,
it is important in all its plastic beauty.

----

* A Tchotchke is a small object that is decorative rather than
strictly functional; a trinket.

THE FIRST SON

Like a cobbler
cutting the pattern of a boot,
the soldier sliced him in pieces.
Put hands, tongue, eyes onto fire,
singed in the village air.

The villagers collected him at the end.
Placed his parts together,
into the shape of life,
the shell of thought.

Organized him into a garden
where scars have names.

FLASHLIGHT
(In memory of Hurricane Sandy victims)

1.
First was the surge, the rush, the brine of the East River.
Sea-swept autos colliding as bumper cars.
Foliage sticking to car seats like coffee grinds in a cup.
The wind whining its tidal howl, a
shrieking angel of death.
Lamps go out, the TV off, nothing to do but listen to danger,
wait for sun.

2.
Later, a crib in the road.
Oil cans lodged in trees.
Crowds converging on the FDR.
Tenants learning each others' names.
Flashbacks of prairie towns where humans
merged like hungry electrons.
Clerks greeted in dark bodegas.
Transformers and breakfronts,
repeated nomenclature curled on
the tongue...
Exiles of the tip of Manhattan migrate to
41st Street.
Travelers searching for family news,
gulping electricity out of banks, lying down in
ATM lobbies, debris, plugged chargers,
a man babbling into a phone, telling his boss
he won't be in, the stillness acute with dead traffic lights;
there are no cars nor buses.

3.
By the third day,
the circle of light flickers, then dims
under the throes of dying batteries.
Candles grow more effective.
A thread of luminosity shines on a cat;
his eyes squint,   .
his nose drips from chill like
ice off a leaf.
I am eating crackers again, under blankets, the refrigerator out.

4.
Shuttle buses take workers to Brooklyn.
Gas stations get guarded by cops.
Celebrities visit destroyed beaches;
televised trucks send in water;
blankets folded under tents.
We are the polar bear, waiting on our ice floe.
The chance of security washed away;
the hoarding of canned
food the only mastery left.
I am happy to have no children.
Happy to die before the century gets really hit.
I close my eyes to the future
like a son standing at his mother's grave.

THE GENERAL POSES

I

Sitting in front of a map of the world.

Pressed uniform bursting from swell of hips.

Tapered lapels adorned with medals over
hidden breasts.

Her smile closed,
just lip gloss.

The eyes discretely looking down.

Fingernails, clean and clear,
rest against the leather wall.

The general crosses her ankles.

Waits for a flash,
as fathers await telegrams.

It blinks,
she doesn't.
Puts her glasses back on.

Dismisses the reporters with a look
designed for colonels.

Walks to the recesses
of the Pentagon,
carpet crushed in channeled heat.

Her language is cleaner than her gun.
And if she is hated, she's hated quietly.

II

She wants to yell
when bloodbaths are flung

at her in classified reports.

She wants to slap the journalists that uncover
inevitable casualties.

But she restricts herself to sadness.

And sadness confines the voice to
grim tightness copying the shut wings of a cicada.

The general turns toward an old man at night.

Pulls off pantyhose in the soft release of a sigh.

Turns to pray to a Blessed Mother on the door.

And then, holds this aging man,
ancient husband,
with the clutch and release of a gymnast
straddling paternal power.

III

She pictures Jesus at the last moment.

The jeering of those scoffers.

That brute ignorance floating beneath Him...
morons collecting dirt and raindrops.

No one believed Him, she whispers...
no one but a handful.

She holds on to this tired image:
the grip of a laborer
as she soaks her feet.

GRANDPA

Face down, on the floor,
arms outstretched like a cohen gadol*.
My mom screamed, grabbed a bookshelf,
volumes of Yiddish fell to the floor...
She wept and Dad called 911.
Later, I got the books.
All with loose spines, yellowed pages, gothic
typeface of Hebrew letters.
I encased the tomes in plastic sheaths like
a guard from Yad Vashem.
A spinster loving the dead.
I protected grandpa's unabridged faith:
the Haggadahs* complete with tehillim* and chad gadya*;
the thick siddurim*, the comments of Rashi*.
I kept the power and wisdom of The Almighty,
trumping Mom's silent G-d, wedged into life like a folded,
satin yarmulke from a Long Island wedding,
locked in a glove compartment.

----

* Cohen gadol is Hebrew for "high priest" of the temple.
* A Haggadah is a Jewish text that sets forth the order of the
Passover Seder.
* Tehillim is Hebrew for psalms.
* Chad gadya (one kid) is a song sung on Passover.
* Siddurim are prayer books.
* Rashi was a rabbi from the Middle Ages.

HAVEN

Caesar lives in a steel cage.
He shares it with Brutus.
They have a knitted mouse and a foil ball.
Their water dish hangs on the rungs.
All the fasteners are anger-proof.
The litter box is shoved to the back.
Brutus lolls on his side.
Caesar sits inert.
They've been in the cell eight months.

Three weeks ago, a woman pointed to Brutus.
She held him a bit, than asked to hold Caesar.
Then, she wanted to see some kittens.
Soon she was gone.
Caesar defecates in his source of refuge.
The pan is cleaned;
women wipe the retreat.
Brutus licks the dirt off his crotch.
A six-week-old gets adopted.

HELPLESS

A rodent stuck between walls
scratching to leave,
without oxygen,
water,
or light.

I was ten when I heard him scrambling for air,
lodged in the bowels of the basement.
I told my father, who hurried down,
then stopped by the wall.
I then said nothing – his bulk massive and gentle.
I asked how the creature would escape.
Dad never said how.
Just stood there,
tapped on the wall
a Morse code
to the dying.

HOLOCAUST YICHUS*

Now a collector, I
highlight tragedy at family outings.
Tell nieces in jeans about
gas vans and typhoid.
Mention two cousins murdered in the Minsk Ghetto and
others who went to Auschwitz.
Add a survivor who fled to Kyrgyzstan and
two who reached Palestine.
It is my hobby;
I portray apocalypse.
Blood ties to martyrs rise up from microfilm
as little gifts.

————————

* Yichus is pedigree.

HOTEL ROOM

You see, the glass door was twelve stories up...
I looked out, saw a concrete platform.
It was a perfect diving board.
But the hatch wouldn't budge.
So I left the room and searched for an elevator.
Down at the bar, a girl talks.
She says she's meeting friends;
asks if I'd like to come along.
She's sweet as a young niece offering the wrong-sized sweater.
I shake my head,
thanking her.
I call you.
Call you, again.
The phone goes to answering machine.
It is 11 PM;
I don't know where you are.

I REMEMBER WHEN MICHAEL JACKSON DIED

In Houston Billiards, Billie Jean stalked the pool hall;
my partner was ready to go home.
She cursed the shrieking falsetto.
I missed Odetta;
wondered why no one ever plays her.
The streets were full of mourners
who never heard of Chopin,
D'jango, or Hendrix.
I turned up Bowery, passed the ghost of Joey Ramone.
The tattoo metropolis of St. Marks.
The lost stage of the Continental.
I passed a punker friend who became
a nun.
On Third Avenue, "I'm Bad" blared from the
cars.
I got tired and kinda cold.
I thought, "It is hard for me to worship icons."
I prefer someone who loves
hard and falls like books.
Someone wretched as a dog
choked on glass.
Someone who riddles his songs with nightmares.
I hailed a taxi through the snaking crowd, started
crying for someone else.

Miriam Stanley

I STAYED UP FOR WEEKS...

Red-eyed, sniffling, sometimes wailing,
while upstairs neighbors moved above at night,
water over a shipwreck.
I reread an old diary.
We were going to live together.
Your toothbrush remains in my vanity,
abandoned weeks ago, a child you cannot afford.
Its blue ridge arched
like your body over mine, glinting near tiles with glittery-blue;
a souvenir of long-lost intimacy,
an amulet held onto to bring love back, your DNA still in my house.

I SWEAR IT WAS AN ACCIDENT

1.
One time, I sent the boss an e-mail.
Attached was a cover letter for another job.
She sat in her office for three solid hours.
She brewed inside like a scream.

What's it like to age in a hospital where
patients sleep on the floor?

I walked out of my dirty office, watched her
pretend that nothing happened.
She told me work on my statistics,
and I, playing the part, mumbled yes.
She shifted files, a monument to fidelity...
Having worked in the same building 28 years...
Ignoring death, vermin, lawsuits;
a woman old and forgiving as a church.
A mute and private spectator.
An immigrant clutching citizenship.
Her name lonely in the watchword of
doing what's right.
Acting as if this solitary aim is surely heaven.

2.
How was it that we got in the news?
Some say an employee "snitched";
others say,
"dropped a dime,"
I say, "acting heroically," calling
up The Office of Mental Health, a
medical Serpico.
Revealing patient neglect and the sexual abuse
in the ward bathrooms.
The Feds circled us like a snake.
Some say my boss retired or was somehow forced out.
Two months later, she died of a heart attack.
There was a desultory gathering in the chart room.
People looked past each other, sizing up bank accounts.
Channel Four stayed outside, talking of corruption.
I thought of the woman the way an adult dreams of dolls:
She had reassured me with silence;
had listened like a priest.

I, THE PASSOVER NAZI

We are four:

The wise,
the wicked,
the simple,

the one who doesn't know how to ask.

We stuff cushions on lawn chairs
hauled into the house.

A sister asks, "Why on this night, do we read a long, boring book?"
I retort, "You would've died in Egypt."
Another wonders why the TV isn't on.
A niece who doesn't like matzah calls up her boyfriend...
hides in the hallway
till I call her back.

By ten, it is time to eat.
My mother gets out potato kugel;
The bridge table is set with
salad and chicken.
We haven't yet read the psalms.
Nobody knows Hebrew.
No one cares about the Red Sea.
Slavery is a footnote that everyone wants to forget.
The presidential election is discussed in detail.
The wine is a tradition everyone loves;
it is drunk with a talk about voting.

LET'S FLY TO TRAZODONE

It's about Syrian civilians being killed every day;
my picturing this every minute;
my sobs freaking out riders on the 6 line,
thoughts whizzing through my head like flies in a Dixie cup.
And it's the pills:
Celexa and Trazodone,
sounding like distant planets,
places to fly to and stay quiet,
not slam receivers like old telephone books,
not make scenes in hallways,
not threaten the fax paper jam,
scaring the Filipino clerk who is now terrified to piss me off.
The ways of acting out are myriad;
a bouquet of nasty, little details.
It's slapping the boyfriend,
yelling down the stairs,
calling the Samaritans late at night,
avoiding the word "death" so ambulances don't show up on the
block,
sirens waking the neighbors.
Sometimes I feel I am Cassandra.
Often my words are too loud, too brash,
but the message of truth burns in my throat like a fever and I'm
allergic to hypocrites;
my head explodes when a supervisor smiles "good morning" like
she's giving me the Lotto,
and at the end of the day takes my office.
I wish I could control myself but it all escapes like doves from a
burning box.
I end up losing promotions and raises.
It's a sadness dense as a walnut in the base of my skull.

LIQUID

You don't believe in AC.
My back sweats;
there was no electricity where you were born,
so, damn, I have to get used to it.

There is moisture everywhere –
the scotch, the semen,
the water skirting a glass,
a picture of your son
swimming at a lake.
He's kept in Wagner now,
to be released next year
for crimes carried out
with a gun.
I say I want to visit your boy.
You pour milk over cereal.
Say no.
Each week I drive down from New York,
follow the Hudson, bearing right,
worm through endless
gas stations,
Korean churches,
Mercedes dealerships
dotting Bergen County.
And now I wash the dishes
while you walk to the porch
for a cigarette.
The distance becomes a moat;
the front door, fire.

LISA'S FEARLESS, PERSONAL INVENTORY

I made mistakes I'd like to bury in lime.
Moments I would drown in bleach.
Turned away from women who begged for the truth,
their arms pulling me close,
their eyes: dark rodents in the crawl space of
confrontation.
I have been a wife's worst nightmare and the reason a man smokes
alone in the dark.
Cruelty is glitter.
You never get rid of it all.
It hides in the crevices even when you wash yourself in the arteries
of some sacrificial god.
It's still there: its half-lives burning the horizon.
I pressed my nose against the plate glass of domestic bliss and put
my fist through it.

Miriam Stanley

MOM

1.
I remember the burnt lamb chops you used to feed us.
The tiny doily you wore to shul*.
I picture your childhood covered in Hitler.
The paranoia on the walls.
You grimaced at Dad when he asked: where should he drive?
You answered, "The whole world hates us."

Your mother was a tight fist.
The future: a house of cards.
Charity for Israel was insurance.

2.
I pour ketchup on dinner.
Prepare for a panel.
It will condemn the settlements.

The UJA pickets my head.
Behind the door, you are crying.
Fear rises in its canals.

———

* Shul is Yiddish for school or synagogue.

MY FIANCÉE

At Rego Park there is a cookout.
She gossips with my priest.
The shrimp is finished, she looks up and
With the savvy of the CIA, crosses the lawn,
Enters the foyer, retrieves red velvet cake,
Croons Happy Birthday,
A Greek Marilyn Monroe thrilling my dad.
She even believes,
Like him,
In school prayer.

Everyone chats.
She cuts moist wedges, serving the old man,
Wearing shiny charms on manicured fingers;
I admire while she — once again the Homecoming Queen —
Reflects the crowd, grins at their jokes.

Cousins laugh about "towelheads" moving down the block,
She sighs, "New York just keeps getting worse."

Afterwards, she slumps in the train, drained from performance,
Speaks of morons, the family she is marrying into. Her words
Go right to the jugular. Her eyes: slits like windows of castles,
Arrows fly out, nothing gets in.
I say, "It's great to have you in my corner."

51

NEW INTAKE

Oversized pants, cloth belt,
Byzantine eyes on a Mayan face,
he steps from a Sally Field infomercial,
weeping about his mother's recent death,
how he attempted to hang himself;
the group grandmas hug him and even the men's comments turn
soft and gentle.
The orphan walks out.
Goes home to his roommate.
Blasts Little Wayne from his Bose speakers.
Eats all the food in the fridge.
The roommate complains.
The teen swears, "I'll fucking pay you back."
Then adds, "My mother was a great cook."
Next day, he's back in group therapy.
High Voltage.
Brought the members candy.
Gives out loosies in the bathroom.
At lunch, the police show up.
Staff demands explanation.
The roommate's bank account was emptied.
There's all the confusion
of seeing a puppy arrested.
But the puppy already snuck out a
side door.
A real pro.

NEW ROMANCE

I wear a red string on my wrist.
A hamsa* around the neck.
I won't speak your name.
I keep your photo face-down in a drawer.
I hide my comb away from your mother.
Go "pu, pu, pu"* in front of gossips.
I don't brag to friends about our dates.
The evil eye kills worse than
the angel of death, and envy gets it going.
I stay humble;
don't fly too close to the sun.

———————

* A hamsa is an amulet.
* "Pu, pu, pu" is an expression to ward off the evil eye.

THE NEXT MAN

He always returned from the Pennsylvania woods with a fresh kill,
along with the stench of his armpits.
She saw the man's thumbs clasp a saw after he clasped her hand.
She shrunk into a corner,
an aphid in house slippers,
fragile inside the clang and hum,
listening to muscle breaking bone.
The heavy buck dismantled like a broken car.
The man was the visitor with the calloused hands.
She was a skilled tailor,
and when she kissed seams together,
dotting with pins,
the universe knelt into quiet.
Later that night,
he pulled off her homemade dress.

NO, I DON'T WANT TO SEE PICTURES OF YOUR GRANDKIDS

Babies are intriguing as sliced bologna.
Memorable as socks.
They are clowns that won't juggle.
It took no brains to create them.
Just drunken codependence and faith-based banality.
Don't brag of domestic bliss;
your Brady Bunch will break up.
Just like Ma Bell, Yugoslavia, and Wisconsin unions.
We could have conquered typhus,
malaria,
domestic violence,
ingrown beard stubble.
We could have settled on Mars,
or in the ribs of the oceans,
but toddlers demand more than crackheads;
they suck intelligence right out of the room.
Scientists left seminal work to change dirty diapers.
I don't want to study coloring books.
Or Hannah Montana bibs.
I don't want to see bubbulas* eating mashed beans.
My IQ would fall down an elevator shaft.
Your gem is interchangeable as a Dixie cup.
I'd rather look at cellulite.

----

* Bubbulas is Yiddish for "little dolls."

NOW IS A VERB

So I'm staring at Frankie.
We are on TV.
In front of Judge Toler.
He wants a divorce.
He snitches that I slapped his mom.
The judge ogles,
the bailiff turns,
then, I'm screaming.
But now I'm awake on a bus,
crying in my seat,
commuters: mute as buttons.
The Hudson: a brown bloodstain.
I shove the seat down.
Despair turns into snowflakes.
My bag falls on the floor.
Onlookers peek.
Some feel pity.
The world moves itself off my back.
Now is a perfect verb:
I now wreckage down my shirt.
I now girls off their cell phones.
I now the driver to miss a stop.
I now the 166 through Ridgefield.
I now my lost co-op over the GWB.
I now myself into Port Authority, with
its abundance of Zabars.
I now coffee into an escape,
into a stolen kiss.

NOW THAT ZION HAS LOST HER TEMPLE...

My grandpa wanders in the Bronx.
Schleps to Waldbaum's;
buys cornflakes.
Enters an elevator adorned with "fuck you."
Washes the hair of his elderly spouse
and takes her to the toilet.

Now that Zion has lost her Altar,
the man is faceless as a sock.

He is divorced from Heaven.
He supports Hadassah through the mail.
His grandchild married a shiksa*.
Zion is filled with churches and icons.
Where in Israel will this cohen* live,
his title: soft as oranges?
He washes the window from the ledge.
The wet towels are bikkurim*.
From the fifth floor, off his living room,
he blesses the wall-to-wall carpet.

---

* Shiksa is pejorative for female gentile.
* Cohen means "Jewish priest" (who is chosen to serve in the Great Temple of Jerusalem).
* Bikkurim are the "first fruits" of harvest. They are offered to the Great Temple of Jerusalem, as sacrifices.

NYU STUDENTS

There they are in their little, purple bus.
Resembling a trolley from "Rice-a-Roni";
demented or mentally challenged.
How else can they not know how to use a subway?
Other times, I see them puking on sidewalks,
coming out of a bar in half a dress.
I was starving and sober when I was in school.
Coffee was skipped for tokens.

The rebels smoke weed in their dorm.
Their parents go to yoga and practice Tai Chi.
The seniors vote liberal but can't find Damascus.
Freshmen research fresh iPads.
Friday night is a zoo.
The kids stumble onto St. Mark's;
feasting on air,
bridge-and-tunnel piranhas armed with fake IDs.
We locals weave through them;
relieved stupidity isn't contagious.
Soon these kids will make our laws.
Some of them will decide our rent.
A few will even kick us out.
We'll be their used tampons,
overcooked leftovers,
the broken blender in the mail.
In the meantime, they argue with bouncers.

OCCUPATIONAL HAZARD

So now there are a lot of teachers at the clinic
who ended up with Major Depression.
Not even "Adjustment Disorder."
Recent starvation, and suicide attempts.
These ladies who bought crayons at yard sales.
They hand out feedback at group.
Prepared like lesson plans.
At night, they cut –
kitchen knives lancing a fermenting heartbreak, drawing it out;
bandaging it, then setting clocks for the next morning.
Lugging flashbacks on buses of rapes in basements;

These packhorses, middle-aged, nodding hello, early for the next
session, hugging the other members.

Miriam Stanley

OFF THE MEDS

She's still bright enough to clamp down on the chaos.
Remains silent.
Sitting on the steps, smoking a carton of Pall Malls.
Heavy, passive,
as her job is taken away.
None of her coworkers approach.
She's a plastic bag of
kerosene and no one wants to shake her.

PAPER AIRPLANE

An origami of contempt,
its trajectory passing chairs by the window.
The man smiles when it hits the glass.
The patients ignore him.
They talk about the clinical director quitting.
There's fresh tears and panic.
But he's a medical student...
soon: a surgeon...
Sits in a corner,
stares at the clock.
Combs his Fabio coif.
The group designs a scrapbook.
A plea to be remembered.
The scholar texts his girlfriend.
They're doing arts and crafts!!
Arrogance suffuses the room,
barking at confused mourners, keeping them at arm's length.
Does he know they sense his disgust, pulling on their nerves in its
undertow?...
Just what they feel everyday, outside?
A taste of their own distraction?
Scribbled hearts, scrawled advice,
Bible quotes glued on pages for a therapist packing her books in the
next room.

- Decency gone in three days.

PARTY IN THE TIME OF INFLUENZA

We each had to wear a face mask.
The kind worn by surgeons.
A blue cotton soft as a Stayfree.
Our hot breath smothered inside.
Yet when someone brought out cake,
These covers were yanked off, the office door shut,
We feasted on slices,
Our eyes gleamed: an epidemic of joy;
The birthday girl was fifty:
We giggled "vintage," "an item for Antiques Roadshow."
Someone yelled, "The half-century mark! A monument!"
The honoree grinned, exposing yellow teeth.
She sat up in her chair.
Resplendent as the Lincoln Memorial.
Her mask went back up, hiding laugh lines.
Two clerks brought out jump ropes.
We played limbo to Bob Marley, the king of Crown Heights.
Meanwhile, downstairs, fevers peaked,
Phlegm sprayed the glass-and-steel ER.

PARTY OUT OF BOUNDS

This is to the insomniacs who never leave.
Schmoozers you want to beat with a stick.
Yentas who hover like fallout.
Stories longer than a Yom Kippur service and harder to escape.
This is to the lifelong New Yorkers arriving at 10 for a party starting at 6;
those nonconformists slower than a wheelchair in the snow.
This is to the brilliant who seemingly can't tell time.
Don't they have jobs, watches, manners???
Don't they have apartments waiting with beds and toilets?
Don't they have bosses, edgy as hungry seals
the next morning?
This is to crusty dishes, goblets of red wine,
Cheese Doodles on the floor, drunks on the table.
I wait...
as the literati, the New School grads, and NYFA gods,
who smoke weed
behind my building,
finally pick up their
pocketbooks and knapsacks to go home.
This is to the ghost of a thousand hours.

PAYDAY

The end of the work week glows...
We wait for our checks in the halls of the hospital basement.
An administrator sends a clerk to pick up his stub.
The rest of us cry about the heat.
The hospital's kitchen is twenty yards down.
We sweat into our shoes.
Psych techs align like Canadian geese heading for Maryland,
Dream of hotels that loosen men's neckties,
visiting grandparents further south in the parishes of Jamaica.
Later, nurses drive to Nostrand,
buy akee at Key Food,
cook salted codfish in childhood memory...
Mourn the inflation of the Caribbean.
The dirty hands of the CIA.
The shortages that chased them into Brooklyn;
their bullied sons in public school
who switch from pressed slacks to sagging pants.
Their frightened daughters with the hard looks.
Later, July 4th comes.
At least there's overtime.
Afterwards, peas and rice;
curried goat.

PEDDLING YOUR BOOK

First, you straddle bar stools next to friends;
shove titles by their drinks.

Then you schmooze the people you hate.
You might as well dig through glass with your thumbs.

You gamble your Yiddishe balls across a woman who worships
Amiri Baraka.
Even Hemingway couldn't take it.
You would take your own life,
but it would embarrass your psychiatrist.
Politeness is asbestos clogging the lungs.

POOL

I learned warped cue sticks roll crooked on tables,
concrete floors are perfect for sneakers,
nine-ball is kind to losers,
that 11th Street waters its drinks.
I found that opponents prayed to mothers the way they used to beg
for allowance.
I played at tables lined up like Cadillacs,
and at dives where six quarters start a match.
I wear hamsa earrings.
Then stalk the eight ball like it's the girl left alone at the end of
the prom,
the deer separated from the rest of the herd.
I angle my hit to a corner pocket,
I catch it like a train.

THE POTHEADS ON MY STOOP

I threatened them with my cell phone.
Promised I'd take a picture.
I wielded it higher than a gun.
I warned them, "Get the fuck off my block."
I knew they came from Baruch.
I told them to smoke in their mothers' kitchen.
Windows opened.
Neighbors looked out.
And you, with your pussy-pink face and
briefcase from Woodbury Commons,
hid behind a dumpster.
I cursed the fleeing boys,
and your lack of testicles,
got out my keys,
kicked open the door.

PSYCH TECH

The sky blooms Bergman grey.
I Google ten photos of fire.
I envision Sweden with its peaks of alcoholism.
I know I have to leave,
to suffer the black ice on the steps,
the pounds of grievous wind,
take the 6 train to a distant hospital.
Have to stumble on grounds, 7:45 AM,
heavy with snow,
placing thick soles inside the boot prints of others.
Right now I cross the kitchen in layers of flannel.
The hems push a pellet of cat turd covered in litter,
tracked out of its box.
I pour the burnt coffee, its smell from a percolator left on too long.
Shoulders ache with the exhaustion of constricted muscle.
I down a cup and quickly dress.
Put on my massive, Russian hat.
Knot the flaps together.
Now, ready for work.
Hallucinations don't stop for storms.

RAMADAN

At 7:45, it is night.
That is when you grab your precious smokes,
drive to Dunkin' Donuts,
buy your caffeine,
run out exultant in the cool air;
you kiss me before you have your first drag.
The rush to your head reminds you of Hiroshima.
During the work week,
you nap in your car during lunch.
I observe the Jewish month of Elul,
beating my chest, spitting "I sinned,"
like used toothpaste.
You admit we're supposed to marry.
But devotion is an evaporating puddle.
At eleven we cocoon in bed,
the West Bank is pillow talk,
you have another go at me,
we pull like the tide back into Abraham;
the sheets are scattering witnesses.
You later admit it is easier to worship in Morocco.
I recall Crown Heights, where
rabbis are sharp-eyed street lamps.
I tell you I love G-d
and don't need lookouts.
I tell you I love G-d
even when I cheat on Him.
At dawn, you bring out chess.
Within minutes, you take my queen.

RECESSION POEM FOR JEAN

My friend stops eating fruit.
Eats more pasta.

While watching TV, I make a cat toy out of foil.
Then, I go to the salad bar at 9 PM for half-priced tuna.
WaMu tanks.
The Wall Street bailout is passed.
New York's rowboat has no bottom.
There is too much thought for sleep.
Rage is king-sized, but the price never goes down.

REDEMPTION, 2010

When you walk to the old model car,
By the East River.

You hold your stomach
And duck low,
Make sure you brought your Stayfree.

The woman -
A dentist -
Or maybe an LPN,
Gets it started.

Your underpants are removed,
And a shot is given that costs eighty dollars extra.

But you don't care...
The tubing,
The suction,
Is a godsend.

The windows are tinted blessings,
With water on them from last night's rain.
They block the chance of being watched...
The door locks are all down,
It is a 1970 Impala.

You stare at the ceiling with its vintage light.
You are intrigued.
Anything to turn away from the baby blocking your thoughts.
The "doctor" is done,
You can almost get up.

Still,
You are groggy.
But that's OK,
She told you that would happen.

Fifteen days later,
You are done with your prescription.
The antibiotics worked.

There was no infection.

THANK G-D,
THANK "LINDA."

You pay the hundred bucks more.

RESIST

She gnaws the iron bars...
scraping enamel against the cage.
She is the prisoner they call "FIVE."
She climbs the cage's walls at night.
Her tiny paws swing her
small weight
as she maintains
her
resistance.
At daybreak, the owners find Five asleep,
curled in the shavings of pine chips.
The woman worries that Five will stop.
That in the dead quiet, her intelligence will slow.

The biggest fear is that
Five will rot.
Motionless as her food.

SEDER WINE

Red as the Nile turned to blood.
Staining Jewish tablecloths for two thousand years.
Until the English claimed we sliced children's arteries.
Then for a while we drank white wine.
But Christians still vanished, supposedly killed for our matzah.
Rumor said it stopped Jewish men from menstruating.
We were horned vampires lurking the ghetto at Easter.
Crucifying babies,
siphoning wounds,
poking one Russian saint
with sharp objects.
In 1946, a child whipped up Poland.
He said Jews stored Catholic bodies inside a basement.
The faithful blitzed us with the wrath of Jesus,
beating, shooting, stoning,
hauling us off trains.
The Holocaust was just the prequel.
We fled for Palestine.
Cursing the cross-eyed angel of death.

SEEDLINGS

I remember when I brought roses to a boyfriend.
He arrived late.
So I bashed the bouquet against a parking meter.
The blossoms rained on the sidewalk.
I cried at their death.
Knew there was a rage I couldn't hold down.
When my depressed mother
killed my first-grade science experiment;
when she hurled the three-day-old saplings
out of their fish bowl...
When I crouched on the floor,
trying to pick up more than just plants,
I gained cruelty...
intangible and hidden in my palms.

Miriam Stanley

THE SERVANT

The fact that you worked since six,
assisting a tailor in the souk*,
matching the threads for hours,
your slight body on the floor like a thimble.
Later, serving a blacksmith;
pumping the bellows,
feeding the fire pit.
Your teenage biceps: billowing muscle,
your shoulders growing bigger and bigger,
the sweat across your blemished face.
Between cutting bolts of velvet,
breaking melon-sized coal,
your mind a flinty pebble
in the cloth of noon.
Forty years later, you live in the U.S.
Your tired body now wrinkled, plump.
Stretch marks on forearms,
purple welts on legs,
scars covered in black trousers
for a new job in I.T.;
Fixing PDAs of former frat boys,
once again you are a servant.
You think of your father – a brick mason;
His family went hungry when it rained.
You look at the company cafeteria as an exotic treasure,
so you always smile though you want to punch someone,
and always say "Good morning."

———————

* A Souk (Souq) is an open-air marketplace or commercial quarter in
Middle Eastern and North African cities.

SHATILA

Civilians were lined up like milk bottles
for the rocks,
the guns,
the bullets.

You describe them like
slats in your own crib.

Horror washes you at sunrise.
I keep Auschwitz with me
while you carry the Nakba.

I expel my rage like an offering
but you save yours like it's in the bank.
Sometimes,
when I pray in my bed,
I feel the dead rising.

SIDE DISH

I am from the land of secrets,
nestled in vodka.

I am from the region of peepholes;
you clutch your cell phone in the dark.
I am from the place you say, "I love you,"
when you are not saying it to the wife.

I am the woman walking
down the street.
Footsteps fleeing your guilt.

STOLEN

Thieves climbed the fire escape,
ransacked the apartment,
swiped the TV,
broke the radio;
the cats attacked the shattered pieces.
She cried when she saw the mess:
Her computer, older than G-d's rattle, all
her poems, never printed, now gone.
She ran from pawn shop to pawn shop,
searching for those missing bytes of herself.
It's always the same question:
If your house was on fire, what would you take?
She imagines herself turning senile.
Long ago, she wrote poetry.
Her intellect locked into Microsoft Office.
What is saved from the burgled memory
but its books?

SUNNYGLEN RETIREMENT VILLAGE

Do not float in our swimming pool unless you're wearing a bathing
cap.

Your garden may contain potatoes,
But not corn.

There's Canadian geese at our manmade lake;
Do not feed them.

Do not move the plaster coyotes;
We bought them to scare off the geese.
The committee has now banned patio lanterns.
If you forget to contact security,
Your children won't get in.

Paint your home any color -
As long as it is mauve,
Grey,
Or beige.

Christmas lights are okay,
But not on shrubs.
There is bocce at the rec center every Friday.
At 10:30 sharp,
Our yellow van drives to the mall.

You can sign up for ceramics at the clubhouse.
Do not grow fruit trees;
Do not install a porch.

Last year,
The Laskis were booted out for keeping a lawn gnome.
Last year,
Edith Montalto threatened to build a fence.

No Madonna is allowed on your walkway.
Your garage may contain bicycles.
No parking on the street.
Our compound now forbids cookouts.

We now forbid streetlights.

This is our gated cult.

Do not talk to the men who mow the village —
Even if you know Spanish.

TV ROMANCE

The day John Boy married,
I cried in the living room.
I leaned against the painted,
plaster cupids.
Their gold lamp shades.
Nylon tassels.
Dreamt of a four-poster bed.
A lucky girl's bloodstain.
Mom yelled to get downstairs.
She had lamb chops.
They taste "very bad" when they're cold.
They're "VERY" expensive.
I ran down, crying my eyes out.
Dad asked why they were red.
I loved John Boy's horse eyes,
and the way he could build a shelf.
His mouth set like stone when he hammers.
A determination rare as tintype.
The steady way he lugged logs down Walton's Mountain.
How he damn near never complained.
When I moved from Jersey,
I was in love with Spock.
He's an older man.
Someone with experience superior to John Boy,
with that powerful Vulcan grip.
His freakish logic and buff body.
We'd share a cabin on the Starship Enterprise
and the female crew would talk.

TASHLICH*

Today, I'm at a creek;
there are wet rocks, gravel—
some pass for sand,
the dogs hold Frisbees,
their mouths drool, jaws fixed;
I am on the grass...
It is Rosh Hashanah, the start of a second chance;
the dogs are garlands around my feet.
The sun flashes;
I fling chunks of bread into the waves;
two mutts dash into the water...
The offerings are gulped in their maws,
down their gullets, into big bellies,
my sins embodied by flour and egg now in swollen guts,
consumed, that whole,
stupid affair with you, Douglas, swallowed up.
It will be shat on the ground, then rained on.
The dogs frolic.
Wet fur flat on their sides like a Marine haircut.
They have branches hoisted in mandibles,
like scrolled-up messages,
like Olympic batons, waiting to be grabbed.
I am sleepy as a woman who succeeded at a heavy task,
and yes, I did.

———————

* Tashlich is the custom on Rosh Hashanah wherein Jews throw
bread into natural bodies of water to symbolically throw away their
sins.

THAT KID

But now he's grown.
Not the victim, more a detective,
recreating an old crime scene with his nephew.
Touching the child's genitals, auditing old sensations,
rehearsing with shuddering muscles and whispers into a crying boy's
ear.
Later he hates those urges;
memories spewing their napalm.
He runs into traffic from the noise and lights of the local men's
shelter.
The guards pull him back.
He is quicksilver/uncontainable;
they call an ambulance, curse the cold, drag his "sorry ass" to
safety;
soon he sits in the emergency room of a crowded hospital.
Large glasses, small skull,
legs sprawled on dirty, plastic chairs,
he's the Rorschach test for the staff.
Do they see a butterfly or bat?
Bruise or bullet?
Two nurses quarrel.
One labels him a predator;
another insists he's a lost soul.
The subject sleeps after a shot of Ativan.
Psych techs remove both laces and belt.
Angst drifts through a passing cloud of fear.
He is a box of sharps.

TO DR. WHEELER

- When you call art therapists "fads."
Faith healers rolling in pixie dust.
Women too lazy for medical school.

- When you are canonized by your interns;
called the Second Coming of that Viennese adulterer
who bullied his mom.*

- When you climb the stairs to pull patients from my group,
when they get the message and don't return,
I wish to give you PTSD.

Hope you get nightmares of painting with obsessive-compulsives
with
oversized brushes.
I want you to worry about rent hikes and low pay.
I want you to thrash in your bed, dreaming of patients asking you
for a REAL therapist.
I curse you and your second home.
You and your stepson's analyst.
Your online shopping.
Your French husband.
Your smile broad as a speculum.
You can dance with drug reps and call yourself "G-d";
you're NOT the queen bee,
and all the drones hate you.
We're not in a contest
and the fourth floor is
calling for help;
you got Charmin on your shoe.

_____

* Freud.

TO SHEILA...

You, with the caved-in voice even the microphone couldn't catch.
You stand behind the podium, looking down;
the audience schmoozes and orders wine.
I was once you:
a crease in the curtains,
a shout in the closet.
Hands quaking during a reading.
You are still fermenting.
Still in the black loam.
Only a shoot sticks out,
covered by forest.
You look through this tangle of twisted boughs, extracting light.

G-d bless your earnest mumblings.
G-d bless your need to pee.

TOP GUN

He keeps the hospital like he keeps himself:
messy and neglected.
With one long suspender clipped on his pants,
a vestige of better times.
He waddles down the filthy halls,
picking a bursting, white pimple.
Nurses inform him of a cot that
has gnats;
he mumbles, "Tell me later,"
then waddles to another ward.
At the end of the shift,
he's back at his polished walnut desk,
with the plaque announcing,
"Chief Executive of Physical Management"
on the oak door.
He unpacks a bagged peanut butter and jelly.
We see he has a beautiful wife;
her photos are in Saran wrap.

UNTITLED

The days running back...
each night the smoke outside your home,
curls of death crawling like larvae into lungs...
your mind filled with the spare parts of
women and their histories...
you are old,
ready to retire,
but sex makes you pick up the phone.
Two hours later, she drives down,
walks across the lawn like an
EMS making a call.
She has combed her disheveled hair.
You say comments about family...
everything moves steadier
than an old LP, the steps done on
autopilot;
you can't even lie that you love her.
She has only known cheap motels;
she asks nothing.
Sometimes you want to be slammed
against the windshield, death dramatic
as the tabloids, the switch turned off while people
continue to speculate.
This is what happens when
you live in Hackensack.
Once I met you at a bus stop
in Englewood.
You were reading Noam Chomsky.
I wanted to ask you about the book but you hid
yourself in a cloud of Marlboros.
Sometimes I want to leave life, too.
Pull myself out of the feudal well.
Get a refund-full of coupons from G-d.
But then I listen to Lou Reed,
and dream of you swimming with turtles,
the Galapagos cliffs black as night.
Flamingos and boobies scaling the
islands' rocks.
History and science stroking your
throbbing head.

Worries blocked by the loud splash of seals.
I wish I can be there, too, like a seed in an apple.
Instead I read of a reporter
raped by a pack of men in Tahrir Square.
Throughout her screams, they chanted,
"Jew, Jew."
There is nothing I can do
for anyone tonight.
Except look for you at that bus stop tomorrow.
Touch your hand with my glove
like a magician.
Share secrets
like peeled fruit.

URBAN BLIGHT

There are black pockets of infection in my pink gums.
They chew up teeth.
They burn like ivy.
The X-rays showed tombstones
whittled as sticks jutting out of sand.

My mouth is crowded as an orphanage.

The dentist says, "You have a grandmother's mouth";
His eyes call me an addict.

During the surgery,
My gums are split;
Their belly carved,
The bowels escape.

The loosened infection drips its yolk on an old man's Latex-wearing
fingers.

Later,
Thread seams up the gums into a blood sac,
My mind into a hymen,
As I hum louder than the drill.

At nine,
It takes codeine to halt the pain;
The bicuspids were scrubbed raw with the skill of worship,
Lips are pursed to keep out drafts from the night air.

At midnight,
Mercy is found in a sitcom where everyone laughs and the teeth are
suns that never set.

WHAT WILL I DO WITH MY TIME NOW THAT I QUIT THE PEACE MOVEMENT?

Fill the house with cats.
Feral ones.
Scrub litter boxes till I bleed.

Get into the zen of sweeping furballs.
Nurture alpha waves and leg hair.

Contemplate deadbolts.
Feel the calm.
Sit in the room in panties.
No anarchists.
No rich radicals.
No rants that the Torah is fiction.
Just the walls painted a pretty teal.
The twin bed as a homeland.

YOU ARE A GOOD RAIN OVER THE DIRT

It is Passover next week.
The holiday of escape.
A celebration of the "second chance."
When those bullied become strong;
I run to you out of the red mist.

THE YOUNGEST SON

"And it came to pass that a mother and her seven children were apprehended and compelled by the king to worship an idol. All the sons were slaughtered after refusing the king's order."
- Maccabees II

My mother coos,
bends to my eyes,
holds my fear,
says, "Don't kneel,"
so I count branches,
the bones of the ridge,
the women crying,
the fumes of the sun.
Soldiers gather pine;
fill a hole with twigs.
They hoist me, a bundle of flax;
the king waits by the steps.
I am a flask of oil about to be lit,
a gift soon to be opened.

APPENDIX

a-l

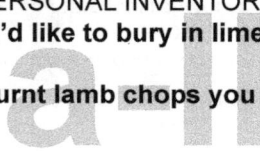

a-IV

•

ROGUE SCHOLARS
Press

For more information or a price quote
for our book design services, go to:

http://www.roguescholars.com

For General Information, e-mail:
mail2014@roguescholars.com

Editor-In-Chief, C. D. Johnson:
editor-in-chief@roguescholars.com

•

More Titles From
ROGUE SCHOLARS PRESS

Awakened
MADELINE ARTENBERG
and
IRIS N. SCHWARTZ

For Better Or Verse
TOM GUARNERA

Out Of And Into The Fray
EUGENE RING

Estrellas En El Fuego
AN ANYDSWPE ANTHOLOGY

Not To Be Believed
MIRIAM STANLEY

Cat Breath
A TWO-HEADED KITTY ANTHOLOGY

Lazarus
JEAN LEHRMAN

The Breakup Of My First Marriage
Bruce Weber

Get Over It
MIRIAM STANLEY

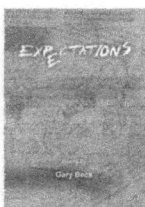

Expectations
Gary Beck

www.ingramcontent.com/pod-product-compliance
Lightning Source LLC
LaVergne TN
LVHW041159080426
835511LV00006B/667